AMAZING NATIONAL PARKS

ACADIA National Park

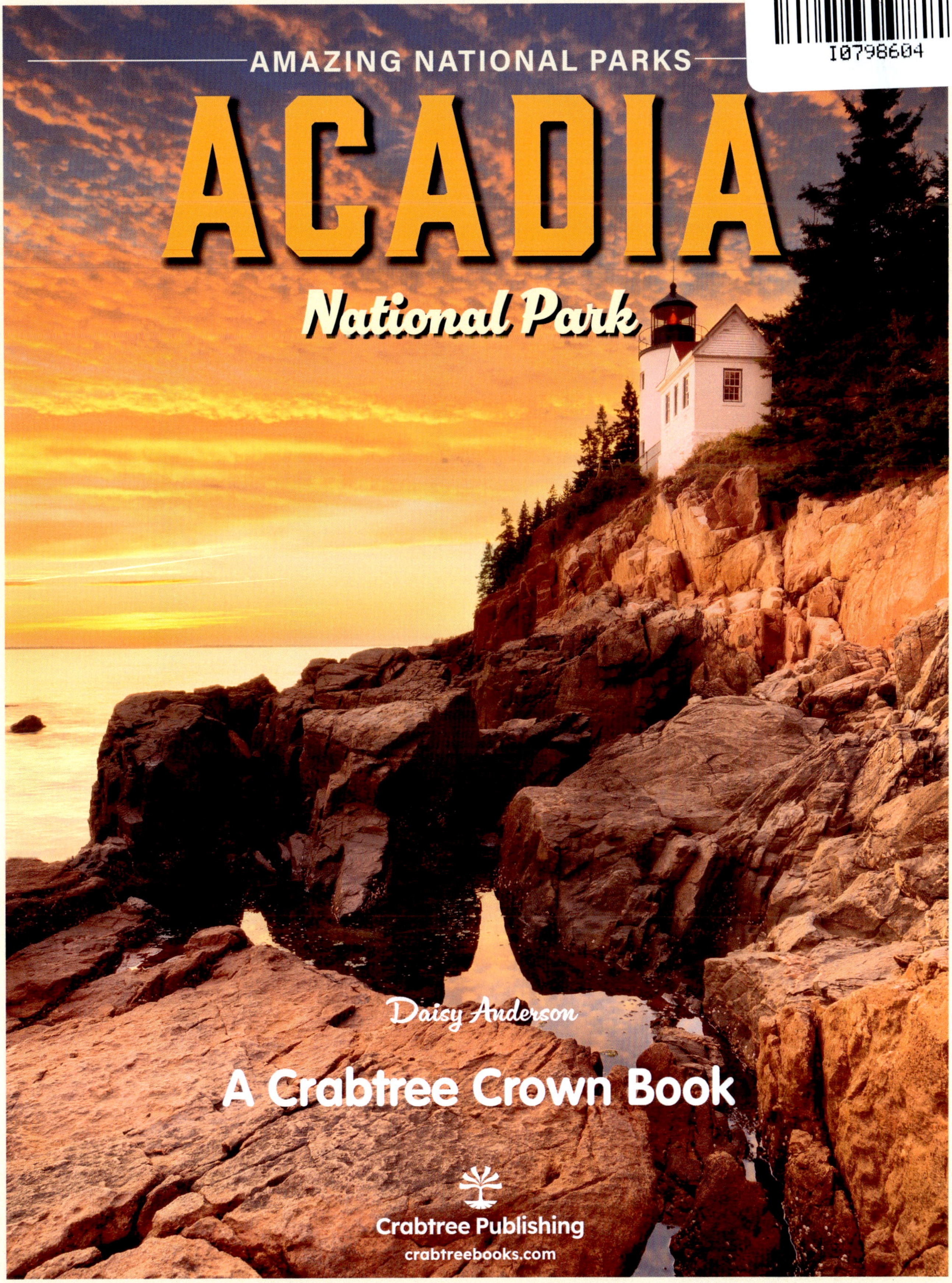

Daisy Anderson

A Crabtree Crown Book

Crabtree Publishing
crabtreebooks.com

School-to-Home Support for Caregivers and Teachers

This appealing book is designed to teach students about core subject areas. Students will build upon what they already know about the subject, and engage in topics that they want to learn more about. Here are a few guiding questions to help readers build their comprehension skills. Possible answers appear here in red.

Before Reading:

What do I know about Acadia National Park?

- *I know the national park is on an island.*
- *I know many people visit Acadia National Park.*

What do I want to learn about this topic?

- *I want to learn what people can see in the national park.*
- *I want to learn what people can do in the national park.*

During Reading:

I'm curious to know...

- *I'm curious to know what kinds of sea animals live in the national park.*
- *I'm curious to know what kinds of woodland animals live in the national park.*

How is this like something I already know?

- *I know the national park has tide pools.*
- *I know the national park also has forests.*

After Reading:

What was the author trying to teach me?

- *The author was trying to teach me about why so many people visit Acadia National Park.*
- *The author was trying to teach me what visitors can see at the national park.*

How did the photographs and captions help me understand more?

- *The photographs helped me picture what the national park looks like.*
- *The captions gave me extra information about the history of Acadia National Park.*

TABLE OF CONTENTS

Chapter 1

WELCOME TO ACADIA NATIONAL PARK

Ocean waves splash against a rocky shore below the mountains. Acadia was the first national park to be **founded** east of the Mississippi River. Today, millions of people go there every year!

Know the Park

The U.S. government owns national parks and takes care of them. National parks are used to help protect natural areas.

Know the Park

Not all of Mount Desert Island is national park land. About 10,000 people have homes on the rest of the island.

Acadia National Park covers about half of Mount Desert Island, the largest island off the coast of Maine. The national park also manages land on Isle au Haut and 18 other islands. Schoodic Peninsula is the only part of the national park that's found on the mainland. Most people visit the part of Acadia that's on Mount Desert Island.

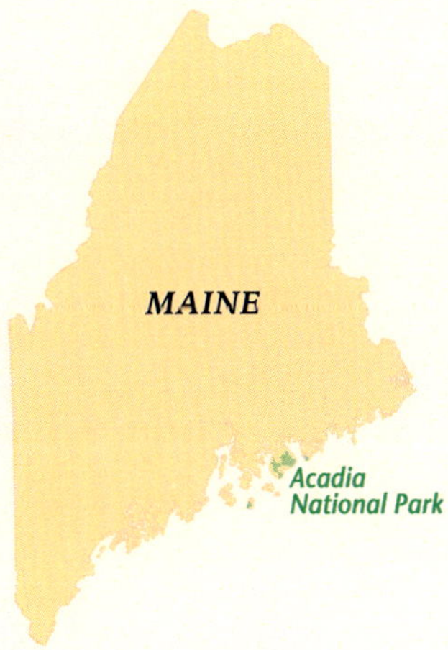

BEFORE IT WAS A PARK

Mount Desert Island has been part of the Wabanaki people's homeland for more than 10,000 years. Together, the Maliseet, Mi'kmaq, Passamaquoddy, and Penobscot nations make up the Wabanaki. **Settlers** from Europe arrived in the 1700s. The settlers took Mount Desert Island, but some Wabanaki continued to travel to the island to hunt and fish. Today, the Wabanaki work with the national park to share their **heritage** with visitors.

Know the Park

The Wabanaki people gave the island the name Pemetic. It means "range of mountains."

George Dorr on Beachcroft Path in Acadia National Park

George B. Dorr

In the 1880s, Mount Desert Island was a popular place to visit. Wealthy people built summer homes there. George B. Dorr was one of them. He decided he wanted to **preserve** part of the island. He formed a group to help him.

FOUNDING THE PARK

Dorr and his friends worked together to buy land on the island. Dorr made many trips to Washington, D.C., to ask the government to create a national park. In 1916, President Woodrow Wilson made the land a **national monument**. On February 26, 1919, the U.S. Congress made it a national park.

Founders of Acadia National Park

THE PARK TODAY

Acadia National Park is the 50th-largest national park in the United States. July, August, and September are the most popular months to visit. About 4 million people enjoy Acadia National Park every year!

Chapter 2

THE LAND AND CLIMATE

The land where Acadia National Park is located was first formed more than 500 million years ago when layers of mud, sand, and volcanic ash piled up. Over time, the layers pressed together and became rock. About 450 million years ago, more volcanoes erupted and added **magma** and ash. Mountains formed.

A view from the top of Cadillac Mountain in Acadia National Park

Glaciers flowed across Maine about 2 to 3 million years ago, carving through land and rock as they went. The Atlantic Ocean flowed in when the glaciers melted. Some mountains became islands.

CLIMATE

Mount Desert Island's **climate** changes from season to season. In the summer, temperatures rarely reach above 80 °F (27 °C). Winters are cold, and temperatures may drop below freezing.

Bar Harbor is a town on Mount Desert Island.

Acadia is often cloudy and wet. The area receives around 48 inches (122 centimeters) of rain every year, and rain may happen in any month. The winter months bring ice storms and up to 61 inches (155 centimeters) of snow.

Chapter 3

PLANTS IN THE PARK

Acadia's forests are a mix of tree types. **Coniferous** trees such as spruce and fir stay green all year. **Deciduous** trees, including oak, maple, ash, and birch, fill the national park with beautiful colors in the fall before losing their leaves for winter.

Know the Park

Acadia's leaves begin to change in September, and the fall colors peak in mid-October. Thousands come to see the fall leaves every year.

The national park's cool, damp weather is perfect for mosses that grow on trees and rocks and at the edges of streams. Ferns and mushrooms are found on the forest floor. Wildflowers such as lilies of the valley and blue irises add color to woodland areas.

Wild blue irises bloom in late spring and early summer.

The Wabanaki weave sweetgrass into baskets.

Grasses and grass-like plants are found in many areas of Acadia. The Wabanaki people gathered sweetgrass on the island for thousands of years but were banned from doing so when it became a national park. In 2015, they were allowed to gather it again. Scientists have learned that sweetgrass grows back better and healthier after the Wabanaki harvest it.

WATER PLANTS

Seaweed can be found along the coast. More than 20 percent of Acadia is covered by wetlands. Water lilies and purple bladderwort float in lakes, ponds, and marshes.

Chapter 4

ANIMALS IN THE PARK

Forest animals such as white-tailed deer, porcupines, and red foxes live in the woodlands. Snowshoe hares have fur that changes from brown to white when winter comes. Park visitors often catch sight of North American beavers in lakes and ponds.

Know the Park

Many insects also make their homes in Acadia. More than 180 types of moths have been found at the national park.

Loons spend almost all of their time on the water.

BIRDS

Acadia is among the best places to bird-watch in the United States. More than 330 kinds of birds have been spotted there. Songbirds, owls, and woodpeckers make their homes in the woods. Bald eagles live along the coast, lakes, and cliffs. Water birds such as loons swim in the ponds and lakes.

Seals sometimes rest on Acadia's rocky shores.

OCEAN WILDLIFE

Sometimes park visitors see harbor porpoises along the coast. Harbor seals and gray seals also swim in the ocean waters around Mount Desert Island. Acadia's tide pools are filled with sea stars, crabs, sea snails, and more.

WATCHING WILDLIFE

Using binoculars or zooming in with a camera may help you bird-watch or spot other animals in Acadia. It's important to remember that all the animals are wild, so you should give them plenty of space. Our food is not good for wild animals, so you should never feed them.

Chapter 5
TIPS ON WHAT TO SEE

Know the Park

From October 7 to March 6, Cadillac Mountain is the first place in the U.S. where you can see the Sun rise in the morning.

CADILLAC MOUNTAIN

Cadillac Mountain on Mount Desert Island is the highest mountain in Acadia National Park. It stands 1,530 feet (466 meters) tall and is made of pink **granite**. Visitors can drive, hike, or bike to its top.

Know the Park

The Bubbles are two rounded mountains on the north end of Jordan Pond. Hiking the Bubbles takes about an hour and a half.

JORDAN POND

Jordan Pond is actually the deepest lake in Acadia. Views of four mountains can be seen from its shores. Jordan Pond Path is about 3 miles (5 kilometers) long and takes visitors around the lake and through the woods.

THUNDER HOLE

Thunder Hole is an **inlet** carved into a cliff. When waves rush in, they push water and air out, making a noise that sounds like booming thunder. The water that sprays up from Thunder Hole sometimes reaches as high as 40 feet (12 meters) in the air.

Know the Park

Sand Beach is also found along Mount Desert Island's rocky cliffs. It's Acadia's only sandy beach, and the water stays cold year round.

PARK LOOP ROAD

Visitors can drive the 27-mile (43-kilometer) Park Loop Road to see Acadia's east side. The road goes to Cadillac Mountain, Jordan Pond, Thunder Hole, Sand Beach, and more. The free Island Explorer shuttle bus also travels Park Loop Road and makes stops along the way.

Know the Park

The east side of Acadia is the busiest and most visited. The west side is quieter and less crowded.

Chapter 6

TIPS ON WHAT TO DO

Know the Park

Visitors to the national park should follow the Leave No Trace Principles. They include staying on trails, leaving no trash behind, and treating wildlife with respect.

HIKING

Acadia National Park has more than 150 miles (241 kilometers) of hiking trails. Some, such as Jesup Path, are for people of all abilities and are wheelchair friendly. Other trails are difficult. The 3-mile (5-kilometer) Precipice Trail goes up the side of a cliff.

TIDEPOOLING

When the tides go out, they leave behind pools of water in low areas on Acadia's rocky shores. These tide pools are like windows into ocean life. Visitors who peek into the tide pools may see crabs, sea stars, and more.

Know the Park

To protect tide pool creatures, look, but don't touch. Stay on the rocks and never wade into a tide pool.

BICYCLING AND HORSEBACK RIDING

Visitors enjoy riding bikes and horses along the 45 miles (72 kilometers) of carriage roads that go through Acadia on Mount Desert Island. The carriage roads are made of crushed stone, and no cars are allowed.

Know the Park

The carriage roads were a gift from John D. Rockefeller Jr. He and his family paid for crews to build the roads from 1913 to 1940.

Whether you hike, bicycle, or just visit a beach for the day, Acadia National Park is amazing, from its seashores to its mountains!

GLOSSARY

climate (KLYE-mit): The usual weather conditions of a place over a long period of time

coniferous (kuh-NIF-ur-uhs): An evergreen tree that has needles and makes its seeds in cones

deciduous (di-SIJ-oo-uhs): A tree that loses all its leaves every year in fall

founded (FOUND-ed): Created or began

glaciers (GLAY-shurz): Giant masses of ice and snow that move like very slow rivers

granite (GRAN-it): A very hard type of rock that is often gray but may also be pink, white, or black

heritage (HER-i-tij): Traditions and beliefs that a people consider an important part of their history

inlet (IN-let): A narrow body of water that goes into the land from a larger body of water

magma (MAG-muh): Hot, melted rock found beneath Earth's surface

national monument (NASH-uh-nl MON-uh-ment): Land or historic area that has been given permanent protection by the U.S. president or Congress

preserve (pri-ZURV): To protect something so that it stays in its original state

settlers (SET-lers): People who move to a new place and make it their home

INDEX

COMPREHENSION QUESTIONS

1. Acadia National Park is off the coast of ____.
   a. Cape Cod
   b. Maine
   c. Rhode Island
2. Acadia is often ____.
   a. sunny and warm
   b. dry and hot
   c. wet and cloudy
3. ____ is the highest mountain in the national park.
   a. Thunder Hole
   b. The Bubbles
   c. Cadillac Mountain
4. True or False: Jordan Pond is the deepest lake in Acadia.
5. True or False: Most people visit the part of Acadia that's on Mount Desert Island.

Answers: 1. B, 2. C, 3. C, 4. True, 5. True

ABOUT THE AUTHOR

Daisy Anderson loves to write real-life books for curious kids. She lives in the Midwest, where she enjoys exploring the great outdoors with her two dogs. When Daisy isn't writing, she's out hiking and having fun in nature.

Written by: Daisy Anderson
Designed by: Bobbie Houser
Series Development: James Earley
Proofreader: Melissa Boyce
Educational Consultant: Marie Lemke M.Ed.

Photographs:
t = Top, c = Center, b = Bottom, l = Left, r = Right
Alamy: Military Collection: p. 6; NPC Collectiom: p. 7 t, 7 b, 8
Shutterstock: Sara Winter: cover, p. 1; pisaphotography: p. 4; Zack Frank: p. 5 t; Globe Turner: p. 5 b; Romiana Lee: p. 9; Jane Rix: p. 10-11; Mihai_Andritoiu: p. 12; MackenzieLR: p. 13; Don Donelson: p. 14; Donna Carpenter: p. 15 t; Katkami: p. 15 b; Earl D. Walker: p. 16; Andreas Juergensmeier: p. 17; Jim Cumming: p. 18 t; Arend Trent: p. 18 b; Harry Collins Photography: p. 19-21; Richard Nieves: p. 22; Jon Bilous: p. 23; kurdistan: p. 24; Nicolas VINCENT: p. 25; Dustin Ewy: p. 26; Alexey Stiop: p. 27; Jason Busa: p. 28; Alexey Stiop: p. 29

Crabtree Publishing

crabtreebooks.com 800-387-7650

Printed in Canada/012025/CP20250101

Published in Canada
Crabtree Publishing
616 Welland Ave.
St. Catharines, Ontario
L2M 5V6

Published in the United States
Crabtree Publishing
347 Fifth Ave
Suite 1402-145
New York, NY 10016

Library and Archives Canada Cataloguing in Publication
Available at Library and Archives Canada

Library of Congress Cataloging-in-Publication Data
Available at the Library of Congress

Hardcover: 978-1-0398-6482-5
Paperback: 978-1-0398-6551-8
Ebook (pdf): 978-1-0398-6620-1
Epub: 978-1-0398-6689-8